www.FlowerpotPress.com
PAB-0808-0187 · 978-1-4867-1575-6
Made in China/Fabriqué en Chine

•FINN'S FUN TRUCKS•
THE CLEAN-UP CREW

Written by Finn Coyle Illustrated by Srimalie Bassani

We are the clean-up crew. We keep our city clean with the help of some really awesome trucks.

Each one has a job of its own.
Can you guess what each one does?

REAR LOADER

COMPRESSION BOX

LEVER

The garbage truck picks up garbage. It squishes the garbage to make it small so we can move it to a trash collection site.

CARGO BOX

CAB

REAR DRAIN TANK

The recycling truck picks up recycling bins and bags and takes the items to be recycled and reused.

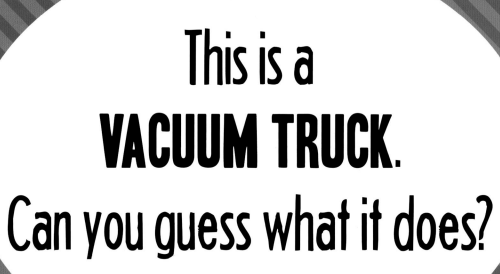

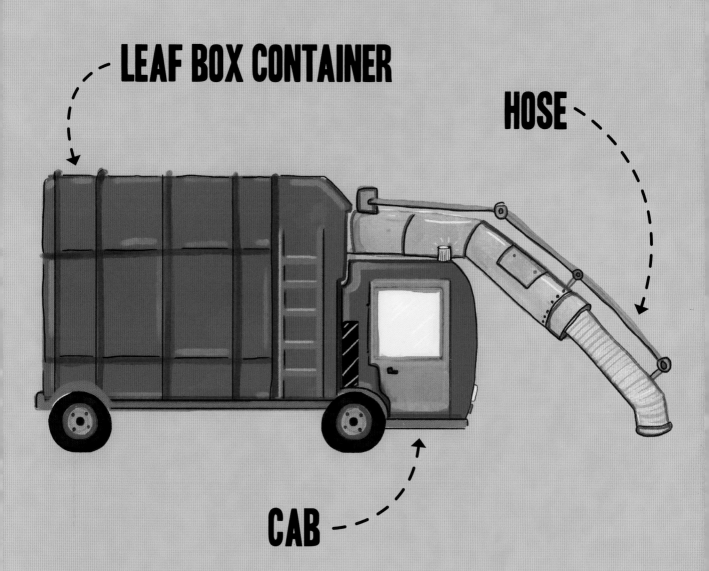

LEAF BOX CONTAINER

HOSE

CAB

The vacuum truck sucks up leaves and chews them up to be reused in gardens.

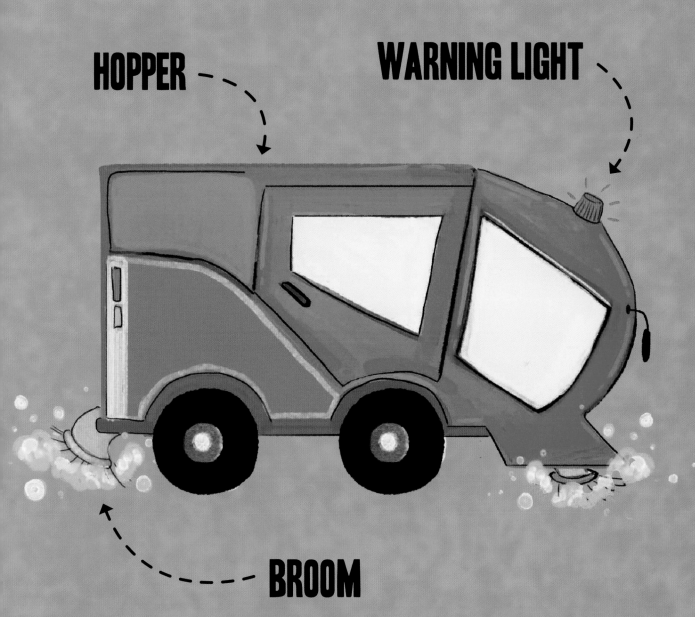

HOPPER

WARNING LIGHT

BROOM

The street sweeper sweeps up dirt
from the streets so they look clean and tidy.

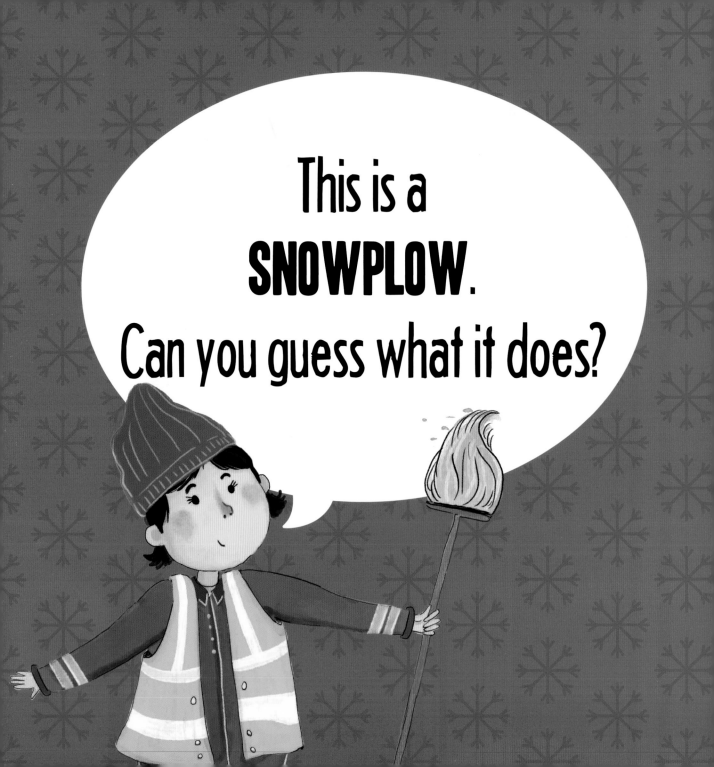

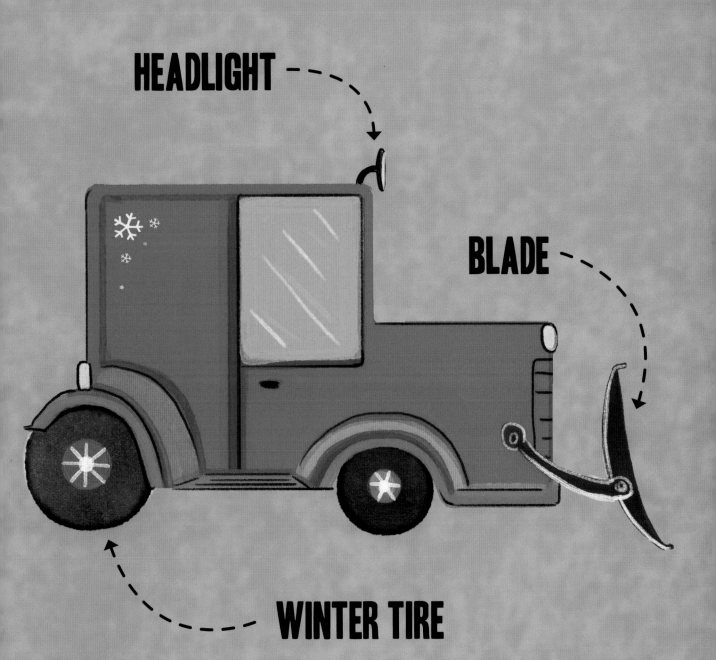

The snowplow cleans the snow and ice
off the streets to make them safe for drivers.

We are the clean-up crew!

We can keep our city safe and clean!

GARBAGE TRUCK

VACUUM TRUCK

STREET SWEEPER

SNOWPLOW

RECYCLING TRUCK